7/21

ANIMAL MOVES AT THE ZOO

Written by Chelsea Jackson

Illustrated by Afrianas Dwi Yoga

ISBN-13: 978-1-7357930-1-6

Published by Spring Willow Books

Springville, UT 84663

Cover design by Chelsea Jackson and Afrianas Dwi Yoga

Typeset by Chelsea Jackson

Edited by Jackson Writing and Editing, LLC

Dedication

To my incredible husband who supports my crazy dreams and to my precious daughter who loves our zoo.

Monkey swings from branch to branch,

almost like a silly dance!

Zebra gallops with her herd.

A hungry hunter must have stirred.

Crocodile CHOMPS his favorite food.

But oh
BEWARE—he's
in a mood!

Flamingo balances

on one foot,

relaxing while she's staying put.

Snake flicks his tongue
and slithers along,
always hissing
his sneaky song.

Tortoise slowly c r a w l s around,

always in his shell is found.

Frog jumps oh so high.
It seems like he can touch the sky.

Chameleon moves from place to place.

His color changes from tail to face.

Parrot flies on wings of blue.

Wouldn't you like to fly there too?

Bear sniffs to find a snack
and stops to scratch
his itchy back.

Cheetah runs in chase of prey.

She better not miss or hungry she'll stay.

Elephant stomps her massive feet and declares her muddy bath complete.

Lion shakes his shaggy mane

and sees the expanse of his domain.

Giraffe stretches for leaves up high.

A flash of color. A butterfly!

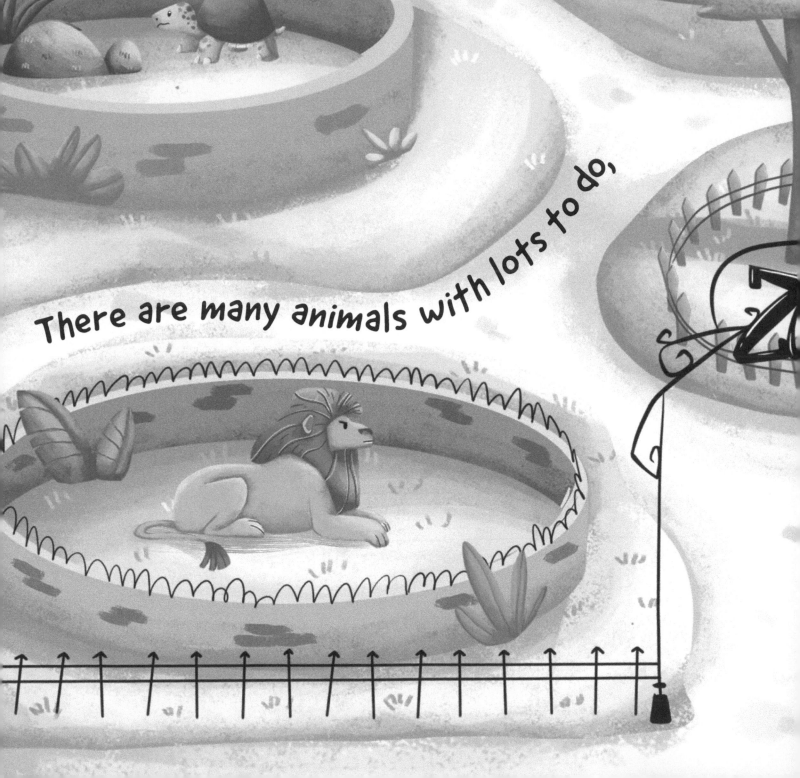

There are many animals with lots to do,

About the Author

Chelsea Jackson hordes children's picture books—and now she writes them! She also might have a problem hording animals, if you ask her very patient husband, William. Chelsea majored in English and minored in editing at Brigham Young University. She now freelance edits children's books and loves being a mom to Princess Aurora and their 17 animals and counting.

Shhh. Don't tell William.

Chelsea and her family live in Springville, Utah.

About the Illustrator

Afrianas Dwi Yoga is a freelance illustrator from Indonesia. Drawing has been his hobby since childhood. He studied at the Indonesian Institute of Art in Yogyakarta.

He loves to teach children through his illustrations.

CPSIA information can be obtained
at www.ICGtesting.com
Printed in the USA
LVHW071938240321
682335LV00009B/203